FANTASTIC FROGS

Facts and amazing photographs of
endangered frogs, toads, and tadpoles

SUSAN NEWMAN LERER

© 2020 Frogs Are Green, Inc.

All rights reserved. No part of this work may be reproduced or used in any form by any means—graphic, electronic, or mechanical, including photocopying, recording, taping, or any information storage and retrieval system—without written permission of the publisher.

Fantastic Frogs: Facts and amazing photographs of endangered frogs, toads, and tadpoles

Designed, compiled, and edited by Susan Newman Lerer

ISBN: 978-0-578-71516-2

First Edition
Printed in the USA.

Frogs Are Green is an educational awareness organization founded in 2009 to inform the public about threats to frogs and other amphibians.

Many species have gone extinct and many more are threatened by deforestation and habitat loss, pollution and toxins in our rivers and streams, and a devastating disease called chytrid fungus.

We provide information through our blog https://frogsaregreen.org, the books we publish, and annual events geared toward children and adults. Our annual kids art contest, held every fall, draws hundreds—sometimes thousands—of entries.

We put this book together to share the facts about these most compelling of creatures.

— Susan Newman Lerer
    Founder

EARTH

Frogs have been on the Earth for over 200 million years, at least as long as the dinosaurs.

Guibemantis liber
Free Madagascar Frog
Photo courtesy of Devin Edmonds

TOADS

All toads are frogs, but not all frogs are toads. Frogs live near ponds, swamps and marshes. Frogs can live on the ground or in trees, but toads live only on the ground. Some frogs live in deserts and only come to the surface during the rainy season and breed in shallow vernal pools and puddles that dry quickly.

Anaxyrus canorus
Yosemite Toad
Photo courtesy of Devin Edmonds

FEET

Frogs usually have webbed hind feet, and some have webbed front feet. Some frogs, such as tree frogs, have pads on their toes that help them climb trees, or even stick to a glass window.

Rhacophorus rhodopus
Red-webbed Tree Frog
Photo courtesy of Devin Edmonds

GOLIATH

The largest frog is the African Goliath Frog. One of the smallest is smaller than a dime, the *Paedophryne amauensis*, which was recently discovered on the island of Papua New Guinea.

Conraua goliath
Goliath Frog
Photo courtesy of Wikimedia Commons

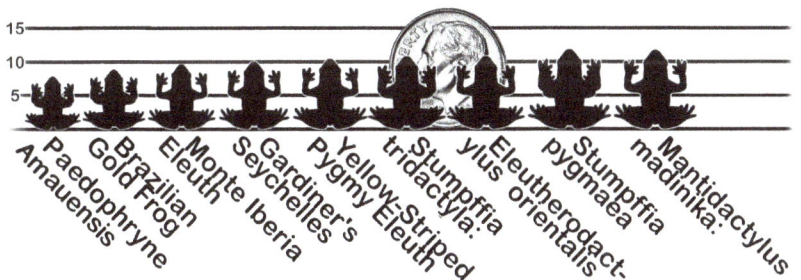

Photo courtesy of Wikimedia Commons

SPECIES

There are over 7,204 species of frogs worldwide. They exist on all continents except Antarctica.

Agalychnis lemur
Costa Rican Lemur Leaf Frog
Photo courtesy of Devin Edmonds

POISONOUS

Some frogs are poisonous and one drop from this type (such as a Dart frog) could kill a human. You'll notice these frogs by their bright colors.

Phyllobates terribilis
Golden Poison Frog
Photo courtesy of Devin Edmonds

EYES

Frogs have big, bulging eyes, excellent night vision and can see almost 360 degrees around. They do not have the ability to turn their heads. They also use their eyes to help them swallow food by pushing their eyes down.

Dyscophus guineti
The False Tomato Frog
Photo courtesy of Devin Edmonds

HIBERNATE

Frogs are cold-blooded, meaning their body temperatures change with the temperature of their surroundings. When it gets cold, some frogs dig burrows underground or in the mud at the bottom of ponds and hibernate until spring. Hibernation has a summer equivalent called "aestivation."

Rana palustris
Pickerel Frog
Photo courtesy of Joyce Gross, joycegross.com

CAMOUFLAGE

Many frogs have incredible camouflage techniques: muddy brown in color or spotty bumpy skin to make them look like moss, leaves, and even trees.

Spinomantis fimbriatus
Madagascar Frog
Photo courtesy of Devin Edmonds

CALLING

Male frogs call to attract the females. Some frogs have vocal sacs, pouches of skin that fill with air like balloons. The balloon acts as an amplifier and some frog sounds can be heard from a mile away.

Platypelis barbouri
Barbour's Giant Tree Frog
Photo courtesy of Devin Edmonds

MATING

During mating season, the male frogs in a group will croak quite loudly to attract females. When a female finds a male croak she likes, the male will grab her and she will release eggs for him to fertilize.

Agalychnis callidryas
Red-eyed Tree Frog
Photo courtesy of Devin Edmonds

SOCIAL

Frogs are social creatures that live in groups. A group of frogs is called an army, colony or knot.

Amnirana albolabris
African Frog or White-lipped Frog
Photo courtesy of Devin Edmonds

EATING

Frogs will eat any living thing that will fit in its mouth. This includes bugs, spiders, worms, slugs, larvae and even small fish.

Fejervarya limnocharis
Alpine Cricket Frog
Photo courtesy of Devin Edmonds

TONGUE

To catch prey, the frog's sticky tongue darts out and pulls the prey into its mouth. A frog's tongue can snap back into its mouth within 15/100ths of a second.

Boophis albilabris
White-lipped Bright-eyed Frog
Photo courtesy of Devin Edmonds

TADPOLES

Some species of tadpoles will swim together in schools like fish for protection from predators and for heat regulation during cold late winter and spring weather.

Tadpoles - 10 Days after Frogspawn
Photo: Tarquin, Wikimedia Commons

TYMPANUM

Frogs can hear both in the air and below water. Instead of the external ear like we have, their external ear is called the "tympanum." The eardrums are covered by a layer of skin and are the circular area just behind the eyes.

Frog's eye - close up and tympanum
Photo courtesy of Wikimedia Commons

BROMELIAD

The bromeliad tree frog (*Bromeliohyla bromeliacia*) is found in Belize, Guatemala, Honduras and southern Mexico. These frogs lay their eggs inside bromeliads or other water-filled spaces in the canopy of trees so the tadpoles can develop. They live their lives in the canopy.

Heterixalus madagascariensis
Blue-back Reed Frog, or occasionally the Powder-blue Reed Frog
Photo courtesy of Devin Edmonds
(Frog inside bromeliad plant)

MADAGASCAR

There are over 350 species of frogs in Madagascar. There are no toads, salamanders or newts.

Aglyptodactylus madagascariensis
Madagascar Frog
Photo courtesy of Devin Edmonds

FLYING

The flying frog (also known as a gliding frog) has brilliant colors, long limbs and its fingers and toes are webbed, giving it the ability to glide or parachute to the forest floor from high in the trees and descends at an angle less that 45 degrees (like flying!)

Rhacophorus nigropalmatus
Wallace's Flying Frog - Khao Sok National Park.
Photo by Thai National Parks
https://www.thainationalparks.com/khao-sok-national-park

EYES

Frogs have eyes with an upper and lower lid and a membrane that provides extra protection while swimming. Depending on the frog, their irises can range in color and the pupils from horizontal or vertical to triangular and circular.

Frog eyes
Photo by David V. Raju, Wikimedia Commons

FROZEN

Some frogs that live in colder regions can survive being frozen. Their essential organs are protected by a high concentration of glucose. Once spring arrives and the temperature warms, the frog's heart starts beating, and the frog thaws out and hops off.

Frozen Toad
Photo courtesy of Wikimedia Commons

SOUND

Male frogs call for females and certain types of female frogs reply. Each frog species has a different sound, some high and some low. Frogs also have different calls for an unreceptive female, an approaching rainstorm, or in case of danger.

Pseudacris crucifer
Spring Peeper
Photo courtesy of Joyce Gross, joycegross.com

EXTINCTION

Almost half of all amphibians are threatened with extinction. In response, the global conservation community has formulated the "Amphibian Conservation Action Plan." Select species that would otherwise go extinct will be maintained in captivity until such time as they can be released back in the wild.

Atelopus spumarius
The Pebas Stubfoot Toad
Photo courtesy of Devin Edmonds

TEETH

Frogs have weak teeth, so they do not chew their food. Instead, they use their teeth to hold their food before it is swallowed. They catch flies or other moving prey by extending their coiled tongue. Some frogs do not have a tongue, and just stuff food in their mouths with their hands.

Boophis ankaratra
Madagascar Tree Frog
Photo courtesy of Devin Edmonds

TRANSFORM

Most frogs start out as eggs and soon emerge as tadpoles. At the end of the tadpole stage, the frog undergoes an amazing metamorphosis. The frog develops lungs and their gills disappear. Their legs begin to grow as the tail recedes. The nervous system adapts for hearing and stereoscopic vision. It's during this transformation that frogs are most vulnerable because of their lack of motion.

However, some frogs skip the tadpole stage! *Eleutherodactylis planistris*, the greenhouse frog, for example, lays its eggs on land. The eggs then hatch out fully developed young frogs.

Anaxyrus exsul
Black Toad (Tadpole)
Photo courtesy of Devin Edmonds

PREY

Animals that eat frogs include snakes, lizards, birds, shrews, raccoons, foxes, otters, weasels and larger frogs. Underwater frogs must watch out for fish, turtles and water birds. In addition, in many places around the world, there are humans who eat frogs.

Liopholidophis rhadinaea
Snake from Madagascar
Photo courtesy of Devin Edmonds

Dendropsophus ebraccatus
Hourglass Tree Frog or Pantless Tree Frog (spider gets frog)
Photo courtesy of Devin Edmonds

COLOR

Some species of frogs are capable of changing their skin color as their environment changes. Frogs have a huge range of skin colors and patterns, which indeed help protect them from their natural predators. Colors can also aid as a warning to predators that the frog may be toxic.

Spinomantis aglavei
A highly specialized, medium-sized Tree Frog, 40-50 mm. Greenish brown colouration resembles the bark of trees. (Great camouflage!)
Photo courtesy of Devin Edmonds

TRANSLUCENT

The glass frog's general background coloration is primarily lime green but the abdominal skin of some is translucent so we can see its heart, liver and gastrointestinal tract through the skin.

Hyalinobatrachium valerioi
Reticulated Glass Frog (with eggs)
Photo courtesy of Devin Edmonds

HEALTH

Some tadpoles are herbivorous, feeding on algae and plants. Some are omnivorous and some are even cannibals. Adult frogs eat their fair share of mosquitos, which keeps them away from us and our overall environment healthier.

Anaxyrus canorus
Yosemite Toad
Photo courtesy of Devin Edmonds

DART

Poison dart frog is the common name of a group of frogs in the family Dendrobatidae which are native to tropical Central and South America.

Ranitomeya imitator
Imitating Poison Frog
Photo courtesy of Devin Edmonds

TOXICITY

Dart frogs' bright coloration is correlated with the toxicity of the species. The species with great toxicity derive this from their diet of ants, mites and termites. Other species that exhibit less vivid coloration and lower amounts of toxicity eat a wider variety of prey.

Dendrobates leucomelas
Yellow-banded Poison Frog
Photo courtesy of Devin Edmonds

AQUATIC

Dahl's aquatic frog (*Litoria dahlii*) is a species of frog in the family Hylidae. It is endemic to Australia. It was once thought that this frog was able to consume the eggs, tadpoles and young of the invasive and venomous cane toad with no apparent effect, but adults will regugitate the young toads and avoid them in the future.

Litoria dahlii
Dahl's Aquatic Frog
Photo courtesy of Bidgee on Wikimedia Commons

INVASIVE

The Cane Toad is now considered a pest and an invasive species in many of its introduced regions, such as northern Australia. Of particular concern is its toxic skin, which kills many animals, both wild and domesticated.

Rhinella marina
Cane Toad in Tampa, Florida.
Photo courtesy of Bill Waller, Wikimedia Commons.

ARBOREAL

A Tree frog is any species of frog that spends a major portion of its lifespan in trees, known as an arboreal state.

Agalychnis callidryas
Red-eyed Tree Frog
Photo courtesy of Devin Edmonds

TREES

Tree frogs are typically found in trees or high-growing vegetation. They do not usually descend to the ground, except to mate and spawn, though some build foam nests on leaves and rarely leave the trees at all as adults.

Phyllomedusa bicolor
Waxy-monkey Tree Frog
Photo courtesy of Devin Edmonds

HABITAT

Tree frogs are usually tiny as their weight has to be carried by the branches and twigs in their habitat.

Anotheca spinosa
Coronated Tree Frog
Photo courtesy of Devin Edmonds

SKIN

Like other amphibians, oxygen can pass through frog's highly permeable skins. This unique feature allows them to remain in places without access to the air, breathing through their skins.

Anaxyrus exsul
Black Toad
Photo courtesy of Devin Edmonds

CHYRID

Chytridiomycosis is an infectious disease in amphibians, caused by the chytrid fungi *Batrachochytrium dendrobatidis.*

Chytridiomycosis has been linked to dramatic population declines and even extinctions of amphibian species.

Changing global temperatures may be responsible for increased proliferation of chytridiomycosis. The rise in temperature has increased evaporation in certain forest environments.

Bufo periglenes
Golden Toad
Photo courtesy of Charles H. Smith, Wikimedia Commons

ENVIRONMENT

Frogs are susceptible to various substances they may encounter in the environment, some of which can be toxic.

Gastrotheca cornuta
Marsupial Frogs
Photo courtesy of Devin Edmonds

RAINFOREST

Frogs are an indicator species about an ecosystem's health. Though the Red-eyed Tree Frog itself is not endangered, its rainforest habitat is under continuous threat.

Agalychris callidryas
Red-eyed Tree Frog
Photo courtesy of Devin Edmonds

ENDANGERED

Currently, the International Union for Conservation of Nature (IUCN) lists 587 critically endangered amphibian species, including 375 near threatened and 35 which are tagged as extinct.

Mantella aurantiaca
Golden Mantella
Photo courtesy of Devin Edmonds

Other books published by Frogs Are Green, Inc., https://frogsaregreen.org

Rainforest Frogs

101 Wallace School Frogs - Coloring Book

Frogs, Amphibians and Their Threatened Environment
Discovery and Expression Through Art (K-3)

Susan Newman Lerer
Editor and Designer

Susan Newman Lerer founded Susan Newman Design in 1994 and Frogs Are Green in 2009. An award winning branding designer, she has designed books since the 80s. Through her New Jersey nonprofit she has authored books on frogs and amphibians, bringing awareness about their threatened environment. This is her fourth book with two others in production.
http://brandingyoubetter.com

Devin Edmonds
Photographer

Devin Edmonds studies reptiles and amphibians at the University of Illinois at Urbana-Champaign. Prior to academia, he spent six years managing a conservation breeding center for frogs in Madagascar with the community-run conservation organization Mitsinjo. In 2017, the frog Stumpffia edmondsi was named in his honor. For nearly two decades, Devin has run a popular website about keeping pet amphibians:
www.amphibiancare.com

www.ingramcontent.com/pod-product-compliance
Lightning Source LLC
Chambersburg PA
CBHW062028290426
44108CB00025B/2821